THE ORIGINAL DYSFUNCTIONAL FAMILY

LATIN FOR THE NEW MILLENNIUM
Series Information

LEVEL ONE

Student Text (2008)

Student Workbook (2008)

Teacher's Manual (2008)

Teacher's Manual for Student Workbook (2008)

LEVEL TWO

Student Text (2009)

Student Workbook (2009)

Teacher's Manual (2009)

Teacher's Manual for Student Workbook (2009)

ANCILLARIES

From Romulus to Romulus Augustulus:
Roman History for the New Millennium (2008)

The Original Dysfunctional Family:
Basic Classical Mythology for the New Millennium (2008)

The Clay-footed Superheroes:
Mythology Tales for the New Millennium (2009)

From Rome to Reformation:
Early European for the New Millennium (2009)

ELECTRONIC RESOURCES

www.lnm.bolchazy.com

Quia Question Bank

Carpe Praedam

THE ORIGINAL DYSFUNCTIONAL FAMILY

BASIC CLASSICAL *FOR THE* MYTHOLOGY NEW MILLENNIUM

By Rose Williams

Bolchazy-Carducci Publishers, Inc.
Mundelein, Illinois USA

Editor: Donald E. Sprague
Cover Design & Typography: Adam Phillip Velez
Cover Illustration: Facade with Olympians; Academy of Athens
    © 2008 Shutterstock Images LLC

The Original Dysfunctional Family
Basic Classical Mythology for the New Millennium

Rose Williams

Bolchazy-Carducci Publishers, Inc.
1570 Baskin Road
Mundelein, Illinois 60060
www.bolchazy.com

Printed in the United States of America
2008
by United Graphics

ISBN 978-0-86516-690-5

Library of Congress Cataloging-in-Publication Data

Williams, Rose, 1937-
    The original dysfunctional family : classical mythology for the new millennium /
Rose Williams ; editor, Donald E. Sprague.
        p. cm.
    Includes bibliographical references and index.
    ISBN 978-0-86516-690-5 (pbk. : alk. paper) 1. Mythology, Classical.
I. Sprague, Donald E. II. Title.

    BL725.W55 2008
    292.2'11--dc22

                                                                        2008021648

TABLE OF CONTENTS

PREFACE

Classical Mythology is an important literary and philosophical thread which permeates society to the present day. Familiarity with it enhances our understanding of art and literature through much of human history. However, it can be somewhat confusing. This little book presents the basic structure of this huge body of stories which involve a family of gods. These beings are represented as springing from nature and growing from the beginning of the earth into a ruling clan with immense powers over the universe and over the race of men, who are their creations and in some cases their descendants.

This simple basic reader will be useful for those studying ancient literature, language, culture, or history. Its organization is loosely chronological, following the development of this mythical family of deities. It presents the Greek version of each god or goddess and also provides separate explanations of the Roman version of each god or goddess. Because the Roman mind and conceptions differed somewhat from those of the Greeks, their stories differ somewhat from the Greek ones.

Terms that might be unfamiliar to the reader are emphasized in boldface type. The notes section at the back of the book provides an explanation for the terms. The illustrations are intended merely to evoke the gods, not to be accurate representations of a god's likeness.

The Original Dysfunctional Family: A Basic Classical Mythology for the New Millennium will serve as an ancillary and quick reference book for any group studying the ancient world. It is a good resource for those using the Bolchazy-Carducci textbook *Latin for the New Millennium* and coordinates as follows.

COORDINATION WITH CHAPTERS IN *LATIN FOR THE NEW MILLENNIUM*

II. The Elder Gods (LNM Review 1)

III. Olympians or Dii Consentes

    III.1 Zeus/Jupiter (LNM Review 1)

INTRODUCTION

Human beings have always been surrounded by events and circumstances beyond their control. Even today, when technology lets us at least predict natural disasters and keeps us informed of political and social ones, we sometimes feel helpless. In the ancient world that feeling of helplessness was also great, and often sent human beings searching for supernatural help. The inhabitants of peninsular and insular Greece, as well as those of Asia Minor, had a mosaic of city-states great and small, and each of these had its own stories of the gods, their powers, and how they could be persuaded to help people. Later the Romans adapted these stories, picking and choosing and adding their own interpretations as they saw fit. They then proceeded to give the gods they chose another set of names: those of established Roman and Etruscan gods who were in the beginning very different. The very early Romans worshipped *numina*, faceless, formless, but very powerful divinities whose will could be seen in the natural world. Later, under the combined influence of the Greeks and the Etruscans, a fierce and intelligent people who were neighbors of Rome to the north, gods in more human form developed. However, there was always a close tie between the gods in human form and the natural world. Gods not only inhabited rivers and mountains, but were also identified with the rivers and mountains. The major gods whom we will discuss in this brief work are all members of one large extended family which began with natural phenomena and which was never entirely separated from those phenomena.

I. THE BEGINNING

Stories of the Greeks and Romans on how things came to be vary, but all show a unity not only between mankind and the animal kingdom, but also a sense of kinship with the entire natural world. Most agreed that the first existence was Chaos, from which sprang various living beings. Hesiod in his *Theogony* starts with Chaos, and has Night and Erebus (the deep underworld) springing from it. Night bore Light and Day in union with Erebus. Then for no apparent reason Earth (Gaia or Gaea) appeared and gave birth to Heaven (Uranus), "to cover her on every side, and to be an ever-sure abiding-place for the blessed gods." (*Theogony* 1.121–123).

Mount Olympus, home of the Gods.

CHART 1: DESCENDANTS OF CHAOS

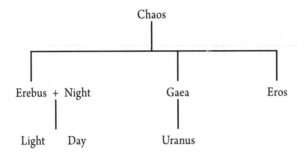

CHART 2: THE ELDER GODS

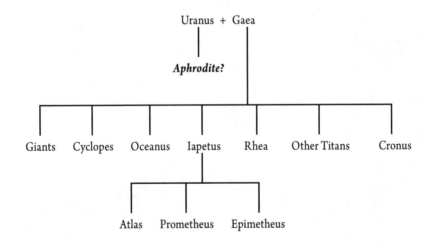

CHART 3: THE TWELVE GREAT OLYMPIANS

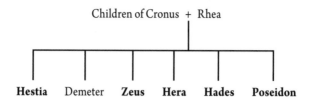

Children of Cronus + Rhea

Hestia   Demeter   **Zeus**   **Hera**   **Hades**   **Poseidon**

Children of Zeus

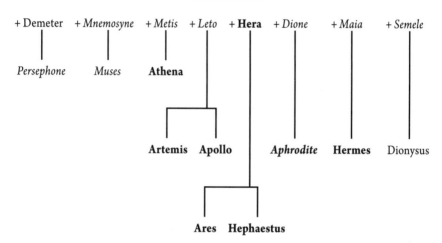

+ Demeter   + *Mnemosyne*   + *Metis*   + *Leto*   + **Hera**   + *Dione*   + *Maia*   + *Semele*

Persephone   *Muses*   **Athena**

Artemis   **Apollo**   *Aphrodite*   **Hermes**   Dionysus

Ares   **Hephaestus**

II. THE ELDER GODS

Gaea (Mother Earth) united with Uranus to bear the Titans: among them the strong males Oceanus, Coeus and Crius, Hyperion and Iapetus (father of Atlas, Prometheus, and Epimetheus), as well as the lovely females Theia and Rhea, Themis and Mnemosyne, gold-crowned Phoebe and lovely Tethys. Last she bore Cronus, who was wily and fierce and more daring than his brothers and sisters.

These Titans, as their name has come to suggest, were large, strong and handsome. Mother Earth's next children were not so appealing, at least from the Greek point of view, which held that man was the measure of all things. First came the Cyclopes (the Wheel-eyed), huge and somewhat like the Titans, except that each had only one eye, which was located in the middle of his forehead. Hesiod names them Brontes, Steropes, and Arges, but we will discover as we go along that there are others, perhaps a hundred or so, with some appalling characteristics. Not that they were nearly as appalling, at least in appearance, as the next three, Cottus and

"Was fatherhood worth it?"

Briareus and Gyes, who each had one hundred arms and fifty heads. Their father Uranus detested these monsters and hid them underground.

Gaea made a sickle of grey flint and asked her children the Titans to avenge the wrongs that Uranus had done to his other children. All shied away except Cronus, who took the sickle and waited in ambush for his father. When Uranus spread down to visit Gaea, Cronus cut off his genitals and threw them in the sea. From Uranus' blood came various creatures: armed

Giants, Furies, and according to some accounts Aphrodite, who will be discussed later. Uranus roared and vowed that his brutal son would pay for his deed when he was dethroned by a son of his own.

Cronus ruled the earth for eons, but he never forgot that a son of his was fated to replace him, and he made a futile attempt to outwit the Fates. The wife of Cronus was Rhea, who in time became identified with her mother Gaea, with the Phrygian goddess Cybele, and with other personifications of Mother Earth. She is described as "daughter of earth and sky, whose chariot is drawn by fierce lions" (*Orphic Hymn to Rhea*). As each of Rhea's children, Hestia, Demeter, Hera, Hades, and the rest were born, Cronus swallowed them. Rhea reacted to this mistreatment of her offspring as angrily as had Gaea. When she was about to bear Zeus, she begged for the help of her parents Gaea and Uranus in stopping Cronus' infanticide. They directed her to the land of Crete, where Gaea received the babe to be brought up on Mount Aegeum. Rhea gave Cronus a stone wrapped in a baby blanket, which he swallowed with no

"I will protect my children."

comment. When Zeus was grown and powerful, Rhea gave Cronus an emetic, and his children sprang forth unharmed. Thus began the War of the Gods, with Atlas leading the Titans and Zeus, aided by Prometheus, leading the opposition (Hesiod *Theogony* 617–885). The Greeks remembered Cronus kindly, and dedicated some of the smaller, older temples and a feast day or two connected with the harvest to him, but the days of his great glory were gone.

Saturn was an ancient Italian deity identified with Cronus, and like Cronus he was king of the gods before he was overthrown. After his dethronement by Jupiter, Saturn fled to Italy, where he reigned during the Golden Age, a time of peace and prosperity which the cynical associated with the time before Jupiter ordered the creation of woman. The Romans dedicated his temple in 498 BCE, and it was rebuilt in 42 BCE and again in the fourth century CE by the senate and people of Rome. It contained the State Treasury and the bronze tablets of Roman law. His festival, the Saturnalia, was celebrated originally on December 17 but later expanded to seven days. During this festival all public business was suspended, declarations of war and criminal executions were postponed, friends made presents to one another, and the slaves were indulged with great liberties.

III. OLYMPIANS OR DII CONSENTES

Now we must take a look at the histories, as carefully edited by the conquering invaders, of the best-known and most powerful group of Greek gods, those who lived in Thessaly on Olympus, the highest mountain in Greece. For the sake of order, let us try to line up the legendary Twelve Great Olympians. (Not that this is easy to do. Some say that Pluto [also known as Hades] and even Poseidon do not truly belong to Olympus, as they are not sky gods. Others insist on including Demeter or Dionysus.) To complicate matters which need no complication, according to the Roman poet Ennius, who lived in the third century BCE, the group of twelve Gods especially honored by the Romans, called the Dii Consentes, were Jupiter, Juno, Minerva, Vesta, Ceres, Diana, Venus, Mars, Mercury, Neptune, Vulcan, and Apollo. Evidently Ceres the grain goddess, the counterpart of Greek Demeter, was in the Roman pantheon in place of Pluto/Hades. Organizing all these deities is a thankless if not impossible task, but let us give a brief overview of the major traditional lineup and take up the complications later.

III.1 ZEUS, FATHER OF GODS AND KING OF MEN

The War of the Gods, with Atlas leading the Titans, did not look too promising for Zeus and his siblings until he released all those monstrous relatives whom Cronus had imprisoned. They not only fought for him with their hundred hands and other attributes, but they gave him the lightning and the thunderbolts which were to be his trademark. The Titans were defeated, and, since they were immortal, most found themselves imprisoned down in Tartarus (the region of the Underworld reserved for punishing the wicked). Atlas remained in the Upperworld, but he was condemned to bear the world (or some say the sky) on his shoulders.

It did not take Prometheus long to dissipate the goodwill Zeus had felt for him while the war was being waged. Because Prometheus stole fire from Heaven for humans, and did other things to give man a foothold on survival, Zeus had Prometheus chained to a rock and sent his own bird the eagle to eat Prometheus' immortal liver by day; by night the liver grew as much again as the bird had devoured in the day. (The ancients believed that the liver, rather than the heart, was the seat of all emotion.) The agonizing liver-devouring process went on for thirty thousand years, until Heracles slew the bird. Zeus, who wanted his son Heracles to receive credit for this great deed, did not complain about being deprived of his long-standing grudge.

As can be seen by the genealogy of the Olympians, Zeus was not a faithful husband. His wife Hera (who was also his sister, as

"The Earth is a great responsibility."

all the gods were relatives) was the protector of marriage, which in her personal case took a good deal of protecting. As has been mentioned, many city-states and societies came to worship Zeus, and these multiple spouses may be the chief goddesses of various worship centers. However that may be, Zeus' philandering and occasional petty behavior did not lessen the concept of his might and power. Homer says of him, "He then lowered his glowing countenance, and the ambrosial locks swayed on his immortal head, till vast Olympus reeled" (*Iliad* 1.520–526). Such signs of his approval, while not as bad as his disapproval, must have made life on Olympus rather stressful.

ROMAN JUPITER

The differences between Greek and Roman gods are greater than modern mythological studies sometimes indicate. As has been mentioned, from the founding of Rome, the *numina*, formless though they were, showed their power and their will by means of natural phenomena which the pious Roman constantly sought to interpret. Since everything in Nature was inhabited by *numina*, great attention was paid to omens and portents in daily life. Roman writers of every era make many references to the auspices, or interpretations of these portents, and to the unseen numina one must propitiate. The priestly college of augurs interpreted every aspect of the flights of birds, as they believed that these birds of Jupiter showed his decrees by their movements. Cicero speaks of birds as Jupiter's messengers and of the augurs, of whose college he was a member, as the interpreters of Jupiter Optimus Maximus (*De legibus* 2.8)

As mentioned before, the Poet Ennius in the third century BCE listed as most honored by the Romans a group of twelve Gods called Dii Consentes: Iuppiter, Iuno, Minerva, Vesta, Ceres, Diana, Venus, Mars, Mercurius, Neptunus, Volcanus, and Apollo (their names rendered in Latin). Their gilt statues stood in the Forum, later apparently in the Porticus Deorum Consentium. They were probably the twelve worshipped in 217 BCE at a *lectisternium*, which means a banquet of the gods at which the statues of the gods were placed upon cushions and were offered meals. Although the Etruscans also worshipped a main pantheon of twelve Gods, the Dii Consentes were not identified with Etruscan deities but rather with the Greek Olympian Gods (though apparently the original character of the Roman Gods was different from that of the Greek). The twelve Dii Consentes were led by the first three, Jupiter, Juno, and Minerva. These form the Capitoline Triad whose rites were conducted in the Capitoleum Vetus on the Capitoline Hill.

All these differences notwithstanding, Jupiter, or Jove Pater, in classical times corresponded in many aspects to Zeus. Rome's chief god had a collection of names even more confusing than most, as the Romans called him Jove, then added *pater*, or father, when addressing him or speaking of him as a subject. This was contracted to Juppiter (Jupiter). In all other constructions he is Jove. Whatever one called him, this son of Saturn and husband and brother of Juno was the supreme god of the Roman pantheon. Like Zeus he wielded the lightning bolt, and the eagle was both his symbol and his messenger. In addition to being the ruler of the sky, he was also the protector of the state and its laws. Since Roman deities usually received extra names for their duties, in his protector role he was Jupiter Optimus Maximus (Best and Greatest). The great temple on the Capitoline Hill was dedicated to this aspect of Jupiter. Cicero called the Senate to a meeting in the Temple of Jupiter Stator (Stayer or Sustainer). His other titles include Caelestis (heavenly), Lucetius (of the light), Tonans (thunderer), Fulgurator (of the lightning). As Jupiter Victor he led the Roman army to victory, and in his spare time was the protector of the Latin League (an ancient confederation of Italian city-states basically independent but bound together by the necessity of defending themselves against their various enemies). Though he shared a great temple on the Capitoline Hill with Juno and Minerva, he was the most prominent of the three. Before the stories about Zeus were added to his biography, he was a very majestic, extremely powerful, and somewhat dull father figure.

III.2 HERA, QUEEN OF THE GODS

Hera seems to come late in Zeus' list of wives, but perhaps because she had long been patroness of some large and powerful cities, she soon became the permanent and supreme one. Zeus wooed her soon after the successful completion of the war of the gods, and after some trickery won her. This in no way impeded his love affairs, and Hera was often jealous and frustrated. Maidens whom she knew him to favor often had a hard time of it, being turned into animals or constellations. Unfortunately he did not confine his attentions to maidens. Zeus visited Alcmena, the wife of Amphitryon, in the guise of her husband. Alcmena bore two sons, Iphicles to Amphitryon and the great Heracles to Zeus. Hera promptly began a campaign against Heracles' life. She sent two giant serpents into the cradle of Heracles and Iphicles when they were not yet one year old. Hearing the screams of Iphicles, Alcmena ran into the nursery to find Heracles laughing and holding a strangled snake in each hand. In no way discouraged, Hera set out to torment Heracles with the same vengeance she would show in dealing with the Trojans after the Trojan War.

"My tasks are many."

Once, feeling that she had borne enough, Hera led a rebellion against Zeus, who suspended her in the sky until all the gods promised never to revolt against him again. After this she confined her efforts to trying to trick and occasionally persuade her powerful husband.

All this jealous rage and spousal war in no way diminished Hera's majesty, however. An anonymous Greek poet in one of the ancient Homeric Hymns (which actually have nothing to do with Homer) says, "I sing of Hera of the golden throne, immortal queen whom Rhea bore, radiant in beauty, sister and wife of loud-thundering Zeus; she is the illustrious one whom all the blessed ones throughout high Olympus hold in awe and honor, just as they do Zeus who delights in this lightning and thunder" (*Homeric Hymn* 12 *to Hera*). Her many temples and holy places were filled with suppliants asking her favor and keeping a wary eye out for any signs of her displeasure.

ROMAN JUNO

Juno was an imposing and powerful figure, guardian and special counselor of the Roman state and queen of the gods. She was protector of the Roman people and especially women, being the goddess of marriage, fertility and all aspects of pregnancy and childbirth. Like Jupiter, she had a wealth of titles. As the matron goddess of Rome and the Roman Empire she was called Regina ("queen"). She was worshiped as Juno Capitolina as part of the Capitoline Triad, in conjunction with Jupiter and Minerva, at the temple on the Capitoline Hill in Rome. From her title "Juno Moneta" comes the modern word "money," as the Roman mint was built close to her temple on the Arx, one of the two prongs of the Capitoline hill. Juno Sospita (Savior), who had her own festival on February 1st, was the patron goddess of the state, and her temple for this function was in the Forum Holitorium in Rome. As Juno Curitis or Juno Quiritis, the protector of spearmen, she had a temple on the Campus Martius. She was the only deity to be worshipped by all thirty *curiae*, the Roman military and administrative units introduced by Romulus.

III.3 POSEIDON, GOD OF THE SEA

Son of Cronus and Rhea, brother of Zeus, Hades, Hestia, Demeter and Hera, Poseidon was one of the older Olympians, and he answered to no one except Zeus (and sometimes conveniently forgot to answer to him).

Poseidon ruled the vast sea, living on the ocean floor in a palace made of coral and jewels. As his floods reached far into the countryside, people who lived near the sea and inlanders as well went to great lengths to keep him happy. When in a good mood, he not only supplied a calm sea but also created new lands in the water, but he could produce terrible storms in an instant. Called the earthshaker, he pounded land and water with his trident in anger, in pleasure, or just for the fun of it, riding the waves in a chariot drawn by dolphins, horses, or, contribution of the logical, sea horses. Longing to be the patron deity of an outstanding city like the other gods, Poseidon came to Athens where, with a blow of his trident on the Acropolis, he produced a sea or perhaps just the well of seawater. Pallas Athena also laid claim to this high city, and the Athenians, who were never slow to take advantage of a promising situation, devised a competition between her and Poseidon. The giver of the best gift would be their chief divinity and their city would carry his or her name. Athena created the very useful olive tree, and won, even though in the heat of competition Poseidon, not settling for that salty spring, created the horse and thus changed the shape of history.

"The mighty seas are mine."

Like his brother Zeus, Poseidon had many love affairs and fathered numerous children, among whom the Cyclops Polyphemus, the hero Bellerophon, and even the winged horse Pegasus are sometimes placed. His wife was the Oceanid Amphitrite.

The Greek hero Odysseus not only blinded Poseidon's son, the Cyclops Polyphemus, but also taunted Polyphemus, saying that not even his father Poseidon could restore the sight that he, the great Odysseus, had taken away. Poseidon would have drowned him except for the fact that the Fates, whose words always came to pass, had decreed that Odysseus would return to his kingdom of Ithaca. He did get there, but Poseidon saw to it that he arrived alone, beggared, late, and in a borrowed ship, only to find his house full of enemies.

When not stirring up storms, avenging insults, or pursuing maidens, Poseidon was quite a construction engineer. Not only did his taking the wrong side of squabbles lead to his building a great part of Troy, but he also constructed the brazen fence that surrounds Tartarus and its gates of bronze, behind which the Titans were confined.

ROMAN NEPTUNE, GOD OF WATERS

Neptune was originally simply the god of all waters for Romans, as well as Neptune Equester, creator of the horse. In the early days Romans had as little to do with the sea as possible, but as their history evolved they not only fell under Greek influence but also acquired some extra-peninsular enemies. As they felt the need of divine protection when dealing with the always moody Mediterranean, Neptune was therefore promoted to god of the sea (as Neptune Oceanus). Neptune Oceanus was often depicted surfing on a sea shell towed by "sea horses" i.e., hippocampi, half horses and half fish (as the Romans were practical even in their most fanciful moments, the front half of these remarkable beings were horses, the back half fish). Neptune was equated with Poseidon and assumed his characteristics, but he was far less popular among Romans than Poseidon was with Greeks, who had a fondness for the sea that the Romans never pretended to share.

When Aeolus at the behest of Juno stirred a mighty tempest on the sea, Vergil says that Neptune raised his great head calmly above the waters, rebuked the winds, calmed the turbulent waves, drove away the storm clouds, and brought back the sun. Then he drove his horses, with their bronze hooves and golden manes, across a suddenly quiet sea, bringing peace and beauty as he moved (*Aeneid* 1.124–156). The Romans, who always kept a wary eye on the sea and never felt at home on it, preferred to think of Neptune, if they must think of him at all, as quieting the waters.

III.4 PLUTO/HADES, GOD OF THE UNDERWORLD

Pluto had an especially diverse variety of names, largely because people were afraid to pronounce his chief one, Hades. The ancient *Hymn to Demeter* coyly calls him the Lord of Many, or the Host of Many, referring to the multitudes of the dead over whom he ruled. He was usually referred to as Pluto, a name which most mythologists connect with riches, and the Romans called him Dis (the Rich One) as well as Pluto and (if deemed absolutely necessary) Hades. He was the brother of Zeus and Poseidon and shared the lordship of the world with them, his share being the Underworld.

Pluto's dismal realm was located underground and was separated from the land of the living by five rivers, none of which were placid little streams—the first four were Phlegethon, the river of fire, Acheron, the river of woe, Cocytus, the river of lamentation, and Lethe, the river of forgetfulness. Number Five was the Styx, the river of the unbreakable oath, surrounding the whole enclave with its dark waters. According to Vergil, the boatman Charon plied his trade at the joining of Acheron and Cocytus. This redoubtable mariner was old, unkempt, and dirty, with flaming eyes and great strength. As he poled up to the bank he was besieged by scores of dead people who wanted to get across to Hades, where all the

"Of death and riches I am king."

deceased of the ancient world, good, bad, or indifferent, were supposed to go. If they had no proper burial or passage money, he refused them; indeed he took only a few of the properly certified. Once accepted by Charon, the dead still weren't home free. He whisked them across and deposited them in the oozing mud on the far side, which they trudged through while keeping a wary eye on Cerberus, the beloved watchdog of Pluto, who waved his dragon's tail and barked his three heads off. He lay beside the actual entrance to inner Hades, and his assignment was to keep those inside Hades in and unacceptable visitors out. Just past Cerberus' station three judges, Aeacus, Minos and Rhadamanthus, decided the fate of souls: heroes went to the Elysian Fields; evildoers to Tartarus. Those who didn't really fit in either category went, according to Vergil, to a number of pigeonholes in between. On the right (of course, since literature has long had something against all things on the left) was the path to Elysium, eternal home of the blessed, and to the left was the triple wall of Tartarus, eternal home of the definitely unblessed. Around that triple wall roared Phlegethon, River of Fire. The wall was breached by a gate of adamantine, the hardest substance known to the ancient world. The gate tower was of iron, and atop it perched Tisiphone, one of the Furies (those female demon-deities who had snakes for hair and eyes that wept tears of blood and who were sent to punish the guilty). From beyond the walls came sounds of lashes, clanking iron, dragging chains, and, as might have been expected, groans. Rhadamanthus, the most inflexible of Hades' three judges, made the inmates of Tartarus confess their evil deeds and assigned imaginative punishments as just recompense. These punishments differed in many respects, but they were all exceedingly unpleasant.

The blessed dead who went to the Elysian Fields fared better. In Elysium, unlike the gloomy grey atmosphere of the rest of Hades, sunlight and green plants existed and some normal activities were possible.

Pluto, as all classical gods seemed to do, longed for feminine companionship. Women were understandably reluctant to receive his addresses, as he was huge and sulfurous. His palace down in the Underworld was described only as being many-gated, surrounded by wide wastelands and pale meadows of flowering asphodel. (Nobody knew exactly what that was, and marriageable maidens were not eager to find out.)

The myths agree that Pluto fell madly in love with Persephone, daughter of Zeus and the grain goddess Demeter. He sprang, in his dark chariot with its rusty reins, from his underworld realm and carried her off as she was picking flowers (a notoriously unsafe occupation which was the undoing of more than one mythological maiden). Exactly where the dangerous flowers were located, though, is a problem. Pausanias (*Description of Greece* 1.38.5) says that Pluto carried Persephone through a cave at Eleusis beside the stream Cephisus. Diodorus Siculus (*Bibliotheca Historica* 5.3), however, quoting from Carcinus the tragic poet who visited often in Syracuse, states flatly that the abduction of Persephone took place in the Sicilian territory of Enna, where the meadows known for beautiful flowers, especially violets, were favorite haunts of Demeter and her daughter Persephone. Ovid in *Metamorphoses* 5 sides with Diodorus and declares that the foul deed took place in Sicily. All sources agree that the terrified girl called on her mother and her companions, but there was no rescue. The *Homeric Hymn to Demeter* circa 650–550 BCE says that Helios the sun saw all, and would later carry the tale to Demeter.

Pluto was successful in his abduction, and Persephone became the Queen of the Dead, the one whose name may not be mentioned (Diodorus *Bibliotheca Historica* 5.3), to whom such charming offerings as a sterile cow were made (Vergil *Aeneid* 6). As we shall see when we come to the story of her mother, Persephone's tenure in Dis' gloomy palace was at least not year-round.

ROMAN PLUTO

The Romans paid as little attention to Pluto/Hades/Dis as they politely could. Ceres and not Pluto is the twelfth of the Roman Dii Consentes. He and Proserpina (the Latin name of Persephone) were known as the Dii Inferi, Gods of the Underworld (Inferus). They symbolized the power of the Earth to provide human beings the necessities for living, as Proserpina was the Spring Maiden (a fact we shall go into later) and Dis controlled the riches underground as well as the Inferus, the home of the dead. Strangely enough Pax, the Roman goddess who was the personification of peace, in her well-equipped temple in Rome was depicted with an untipped spear, holding an olive twig in her hand and the young Pluto in her arm. Whether the Romans thought that Pluto God of Riches or Pluto God of the Dead was connected with peace they left unspecified.

The Romans associated Pluto with the least appealing aspects of their terrain. Near the shrine of Apollo at Cumae lie Lake Avernus and the Burning Fields, two forbidding and extremely smelly geographical features involving boiling mud, spewing gases, and the yellow fluorescence and strong odor of abundant sulfur. This dismal spot was proclaimed to be an entrance to Hades, the World of the Dead.

III. 5 HESTIA, GODDESS OF THE HEARTH

"The house must have a fire."

Hestia, the Greek goddess of the hearth or fireplace, was the sister of Zeus, Hera, Poseidon, and Pluto, but her history was one step more outlandish than her siblings. The firstborn offspring of Cronus and Rhea, she was the first to be swallowed by Cronus and the last to be given back; thus she was known as the first and the last of his children. (This is sometimes said to be the reason why the Greeks gave her offerings at the beginning and the end of their meals.)

However difficult her beginning, she was central to Greek life; the hearth or fireplace which was her special domain was the all-important source of warmth and light and cooking and the symbol of the home and of life itself. Each newborn child was carried around her fire before being received into the family. Hestia was no less important in civic life: each city had a public hearth sacred to her, where the fire was never allowed to go out. If a colony was to be founded, the colonists carried with them coals from the hearth of the mother city with which to kindle the fire on the new city's hearth, which they promptly dedicated to Hestia.

Plato makes Socrates say (*Phaedrus* 246e) that when Zeus and all the other Olympians go out to wage a war, Hestia alone remains in the house of the gods. Rather than having temples of her own, Hestia was honored by the fire placed in every temple (*Homeric Hymn* 5). *Homeric Hymn* 29 extols her importance and invokes her aid. "Hestia, in the high places of all, both immortal gods and men who walk on earth, you hold the highest honor: your portion and your right is glorious indeed. For there are no mortal banquets where one does not duly pour a libation of sweet wine to Hestia both first and last . . . Hestia, holy and dear, come and dwell in this glorious house in friendship . . . being aware of the noble actions of men, increase their wisdom and their strength."

ROMAN VESTA

Vesta, Hestia's counterpart, was one of the most popular and mysterious goddesses of the Roman pantheon. Not much is known of her origin, except that she was goddess of the hearth, which was the center of the Roman home. Every day, during a meal, Romans threw a small cake on the fire for Vesta. Good luck was assured if it burned with a crackle, so wise housewives probably chose its ingredients to assure that it would.

The worship of Vesta, like much of Roman worship, originated in the home, but quite early her worship evolved into a state cult set up by King Numa Pompilius (715–673 BCE). He established the Vestal Virgins (Livy *Ab Urbe Conditā* 1.20) to keep her home fire burning, as she was protector of the sacred flame which was said to have been brought from Troy to Italy by the hero Aeneas. This fire was relit every March 1st from a coal of the old one and had to be kept alight all year. In her shrine was also the sacred Palladium, a small wooden statue of Minerva, which Aeneas supposedly brought from Troy. According to legend, if anything ever happened to either of these, disaster would fall on Rome. The worship of Vesta declined after Constantine adopted Christianity as the state religion, and in 382 CE Gratian (one of the less successful later Emperors) confiscated the Atrium Vestae. Disaster did indeed fall on Rome, but this probably had more to do with Gratian's policies than with Vesta's sacred fire.

Vesta was a quiet well-behaved goddess, never joining in the endless arguments and fights of the other gods. When Bacchus/Liber demanded a spot among the Dii Consentes, Vesta gave him hers. She had probably had more than enough of that august but boisterous assembly.

III.6 ARES, GOD OF WAR

Ares, son of Zeus and Hera, was a favorite with neither of them. He was tall, handsome and athletic, but also aggressive and bloodthirsty, and he liked to exercise his prowess in that most destructive of games, war. Ares was the favored lover of Aphrodite (with whom he shared a total disregard for the opinions and rights of others, such as her husband Hephaestus). Perhaps their mutual attraction arose because love and war are opposites, or perhaps because they often resemble each other. However that may have been, they had several offspring, such as Deimos (Fear), Phobos (Terror), and the troublesome little archer Eros/Cupid/Amor.

"Let loose the dogs of war."

Strong and terrible he might be, but Ares was not invulnerable. When Aphrodite attempted to defend her son Aeneas during the Trojan War, Ares charged into the fray to help her, with his horses, Flame and Terror, pulling his war chariot. Athena, whose sympathies lay with the Greeks, threw a huge boulder at him which knocked him senseless. When he retreated to Mount Olympus his father, Zeus, commanded Paean the all-healer to cure his wound, but said "To me you are most hateful of all the gods of Olympus"(Homer *Iliad* 5.889).

Because of his prowess he was worshipped throughout Greece, and great Greek warriors were often said to be his sons. Honored especially by warriors, he was one of the first divinities worshipped in Athens, being associated with Theseus' defeat of the Amazons.

ROMAN MARS

Mars, the son of Jupiter and Juno, was one of the most prominent Roman gods. In early Roman history Mars was a god of spring, embodying growth and fertility in nature. He was also the protector of cattle. He is mentioned as a chthonic god, which may explain why he became a god of death and finally a god of war. His sacred animals are the wolf and the woodpecker (which may be a noisy bird, but is more attractive than Ares' vulture). He is accompanied by Fuga and Timor, the personifications of flight and fear. He is portrayed as a warrior in full battle armor, wearing a crested helmet and bearing a shield. The old Roman god Quirinus, who seems to have started out in charge of war, was worshipped separately but often identified either with Mars or with Romulus, son of Mars and the legendary founder of Rome. Mars shared with Minerva a festival called the Quinquatrus, a five-day celebration during the vernal equinox, at the end of which was the Tubilustrium on March 23, on which weapons and war trumpets were cleansed. Mars' special priest was called the *flamen Martialis*, but there were also priests of Mars, whom he shared with his archaic counterpart Quirinus, called the *Salii* (jumpers), because of the procession through the streets of the city in which they jumped the entire way singing the *Carmen Saliare*. The *suovetaurilia*, a sacrifice of a pig (*sus*), a ram (*ovis*) and a bull (*taurus*), was a very ancient rite in which the Romans invoked Mars to bless and purify the land.

III.7 PHOEBUS APOLLO, GOD OF THE SUN

Apollo and his twin sister, Artemis, products of one of Zeus' amours, were born to Latona or Leto on the island of Delos, a barren and unattractive little island which wasn't even anchored, but tossed around in the sea. Leto, an outcast because earth and heaven feared the jealous wifely rage of Hera, approached this bit of terra not very firma as she wandered about growing closer and closer to her delivery time. Goddess and island had a little chat, the upshot of which was Leto's promise that her prospective son Apollo would not despise the barren little isle, but on the

Thoughtful young god.

contrary would have a great shrine there if it were to be his birthplace. As the little island offered a welcome to the distressed mother-to-be, four pillars immediately rose from the bottom of the sea and anchored it forever, and the welfare of both pregnant lady and despised island were assured (*Homeric Hymn to Apollo* 51–88).

In Greece and in Rome Phoebus Apollo had only one name (or pair of names), but he had multiple duties. He became god of the sun (a post which Homer indicates that he usurped from the older Helios) light, truth, music, and medicine. When only a few days old, Apollo slew the serpent Python which lived at Delphi beside the Castalian Spring, and took over the shrine of Delphi. There he revealed truth to mortals through his priestess the Pythia, who became the most famous and respected oracle in the ancient world. As she always prophesied in a state of frenzy, priests of Apollo were standing nearby ready to interpret her ravings as the enigmatic prophecies of the god. These interpretations were often capable of being interpreted in two exactly opposite ways, a fact which may have been of minimal help to worshippers, but which helped maintain the oracle's reputation for infallibility.

Apollo was often accompanied by the nine Muses, the children of Zeus and Mnemosyne or Memory. These goddesses who inspire and preside over the arts and sciences were Calliope: eloquence and heroic poetry; Clio: history; Erato: lyric and amatory poetry; Euterpe: music; Melpomene: tragedy: Polyhymnia: lyric poetry; Terpsichore: dance and choral song; Thalia: comedy; and Urania: astronomy.

ROMAN APOLLO

In Roman religion, Apollo was worshiped in various forms. His chief role was as a god of healing and of prophecy. He was clothed in all the splendor proper to the god of light of the world. Ovid in the story of Phaethon pictures him clothed in purple and seated on a throne carved of a vast emerald, wearing the rays of the sun as his crown. In art he was portrayed as the perfection of youth and beauty. One of the most celebrated depictions of him is the Apollo Belvedere, a marble statue in the belvedere of the Vatican Palace. According to some legends Apollo and Iris, goddess of the rainbow, were parents of the door god Janus, guardian to the Roman peoples.

Apollo was also responsible for the famous Cumaean Sibyl. There were ten Sibyls, or prophetesses of Apollo, scattered throughout the classical Mediterranean World, but the most respected of these in Italy lived at Cumae near Naples. Apollo fell in love with her, and she asked to live as many years as she could hold grains of sand in her hands. He granted her wish, but when she was unwise enough to deny him her favors, he refused to attach eternal youth to her years and she grew incredibly shriveled and longed for death. This aged seer was not only the greatest of Apollo's Italian minions but apparently the laziest. She wrote her prophecies on leaves, and if no one came to her cave to collect them, they were scattered by winds and never read. Evidently at some point some of these complex enigmatic verses, called "Sibylline Leaves," were bound into books. The Sibyl herself in a burst of energy brought to Rome nine volumes of these prophecies, which she said contained the future of the world, offering them to King Tarquin Superbus at an outrageous price. He scoffed, and she immediately burned three volumes, offering the remaining six at the same high price. Again he refused. She burned three more volumes, and once more asked the original price. By this time Tarquin was wondering if he had been a bit hasty, and he purchased the remaining Sibylline books, which were carefully kept in the Capitoline Temple and consulted by the Senate when catastrophe threatened. Some were destroyed by fire in 83 BCE while the rest (or, according to some scholars, copies collected from similar oracles) survived until 405 CE, when they perished in one of those ubiquitous fires. After this second fire Romans searched the world for replacements for the Sibylline Leaves. The Sibyl herself, it was discovered, had vanished. So the way was left clear for the production of pseudo-Sibylline prophecies, which enterprising souls kept supplying until the end of the Roman Empire.

Like all the other gods, Apollo had his good moods and his bad moods. He played a golden lyre, but he also shot arrows from a silver bow, evidently with unsettling accuracy, as he is called the Far Shooter. The Roman poet Horace says, with a philosophical shrug, "Sometimes Apollo plays the lyre; sometimes he bends the bow" (*Odes* 2.10.16–20).

III.8 ARTEMIS, GODDESS OF THE MOON AND HUNTING

Apollo's twin Artemis was said to have been born before him. Some legends even credit her with helping deliver her twin. As Apollo was the sun god, largely replacing the older Helios, Artemis became goddess of the moon, gaining that goddess' name of Selene and often being depicted wearing a crescent moon over her forehead. However, she was chiefly goddess of the wilderness, the hunt and wild animals, armed with bow and arrows made by Hephaestus and the Cyclopes. Like her brother she had a multi-faceted personality; she both hunted and protected wild animals. At an early age (in one legend she was three years old) Artemis like her aunt Hestia

A maiden fair and free.

asked her father Zeus to grant her eternal virginity. When she took up outdoor sports, she was accompanied by a train of nymphs, who like her were sworn to chastity. As Artemis was fierce in protecting her own chastity, so she expected the same from her followers. Thus came about the sad fate of Artemis' nymph Callisto, who, having received no sympathy from the goddess after being outwitted by Zeus, wound up a constellation.

Like Zeus, Artemis seems to have decorated the sky with those unfortunate enough to love her. When the giant hunter Orion tried to make love to Artemis, she killed him with her bow and arrows and added one more constellation to the heavens. An even more star-studded version of this legend says that the offended goddess conjured up a scorpion which killed Orion and his dog. The scorpion was then transformed into the constellation Scorpio, Orion became the constellation which bears his name, and his dog became Sirius, the dogstar.

Artemis also gave short shrift to anyone mistreating her sacred animals, as Agamemnon discovered just before setting out to wage the Trojan War when he or some of his men killed a stag in her sacred grove. His ships were becalmed, and the seer Calchas said that Artemis would bring back the winds only if Agamemnon sacrificed his daughter Iphigenia. Some myths say he did sacrifice Iphigenia, others that Artemis put a deer in her place and took Iphigenia away as her priestess.

Artemis was always a goddess of contradictions; although the arrows of Artemis brought women sudden death while they were giving birth, she was the guardian of young things, and the protectress of women in labor. Perhaps this association with childbirth explains why Artemis, the virgin goddess of hunting and wildlife, running lightly in her silver sandals carrying her bow and arrows, underwent a major change in Asia Minor. The cult statues of the Ephesian Artemis are those of a fertility goddess.

As has been mentioned, Artemis was confused with Selene, the moon goddess, as her brother Apollo superseded Selene's brother Helios. Selene originally was a young woman dressed in a robe, not hunting gear, who wore a crescent moon on her forehead and carried a torch. The most famous story about her is that she fell in love with a young shepherd named Endymion and kept him sleeping forever in a cave so that she could visit him at night, a tale which certainly does not fit in with Artemis' maiden status.

Getting mixed up with Selene was bad enough. Even more appalling was Artemis' identification with another goddess left over from the Titan age, Hecate. This dread goddess of the crossroads was not only usually accompanied by her two ghost hounds, but also was sometimes depicted as having three heads, one of a dog, one of a snake, and one of a horse. (This bizarre anatomy enabled her to look three ways at once and keep abreast of affairs. Hence she was to be found at the spot where three roads meet, with each of her watchful heads facing in a certain direction.) The natural habitat of this unsightly goddess of ghosts and queen of witches was Hades, and when Persephone was kidnapped by Pluto, Hecate befriended the captured and bewildered girl. The ancient *Homeric Hymn to Demeter* explains that "tenderhearted Hecate" heard the maiden's cries. (Tenderhearted toward wronged females, be they maidens like Persephone or witches like her servants Circe and Medea, she undoubtedly was, but the revenge she took on their masculine tormentors was a different matter.)

Some scholars try to bring a bit of order into all this chaos by identifying Artemis as the waxing moon or maiden, Selene as the full moon or matron, and Hecate as the waning moon, the dark of the moon, or the crone.

ROMAN DIANA

Diana, twin sister of Apollo, was goddess of the moon; her name is possibly derived from *diviana* (the shining one). First and foremost, however, she was the protector of wild animals and forests. Under Greek influence she was equated with Artemis whom she resembled closely, not only as huntress and moon divinity but also as a goddess of fertility who could give women both fertility and easy births. She was essentially a goddess of the woodlands: her sanctuaries were commonly in groves; all groves, especially those of oak, were sacred to her. She was praised for her youthful strength, athletic grace, beauty, and especially her hunting skills. With two other deities, Egeria the water nymph, her servant and assistant midwife, and Virbius, a woodland Italian divinity, she made up one of those trinities the Romans found so appealing.

She had a train of virgin nymphs, some of whom, such as Camilla, indulged not only in hunting but in warfare. Powerless to keep her followers from the perils of war, Diana made very sure that those who killed the girls paid for it. She was typically depicted as a young huntress, usually carrying a bow and arrows, which like her brother she could use with devastating accuracy.

III.9 APHRODITE, GODDESS OF LOVE

All Olympians could cause mischief, but none on quite so grand a scale as the Goddess of Love. From the moment Aphrodite (foam-born) rose naked from the sea on a scallop shell she was trouble. Homer makes her the daughter of Zeus and Dione, who shared an oracle at Dodona. However this may have been, she made her way to Olympus and was welcomed there, especially by the masculine contingent.

As the goddess of love, beauty, and fertility, Aphrodite was concerned with promoting the first two to bring about the third, and what happened to hapless humans (and gods) along the path to her objective never worried her. Her principal seats remained on the outlying islands. Her roses, myrtle trees, doves, and sparrows were a bit incongruous in intellectual Athens and certainly did not seem at home in militaristic Sparta.

Pausanias says the Spartans did their best with her, making statues of her dressed for battle. A tenuous understanding between her and the military Spartans might have developed because Ares, the war god, was her lover. In Sparta she showed her swift and wide-ranging vengeance.

"Love will conquer all."

According to Stesichorus (*Fragment* 192: *the Palinode*), the Spartan king Tyndareus forgot her when he made sacrifices to all the gods. Aphrodite arranged for Zeus to see Leda, the beautiful queen of Sparta, bathing in the river Eurotas. Only pausing to change himself into a white swan, he swooped down, and the result was rather confusing. The stories say that Leda brought forth two eggs. One, for which Zeus was responsible, produced Helen (the future Helen of Troy) and her brother Pollux. From the other came Castor and Clytemnestra, future Queen of Mycenae. As the last two were the children of her husband Tyndareus, they were mortal. As the children grew up, Tyndareus married Clytemnestra off very respectably to Agamemnon King of Mycenae, and turned to the thorny problem of a husband for Helen, the devastatingly beautiful production of Egg Number One. Kings, nobles, and upstarts descended on Tyndareus demanding Helen's hand in marriage. Before he named Menelaus King of Sparta as the lucky man, Tyndareus made all the hopefuls swear to support Helen's husband in the quarrels that were extremely likely to arise concerning her. Every man, modestly expecting to be the winner, happily swore the oath, and the stage was set for the Trojan War.

Things moved relatively smoothly until Eris, goddess of Discord, did not receive an invitation to the wedding of Peleus and Thetis. The angry goddess of Discord tossed on a banquet table on Mount Olympus a golden apple inscribed "For the Most Beautiful." Aphrodite naturally claimed it but Hera, who took her title of Queen of Heaven very seriously, thought she had a right to everything, and Athena, who as goddess of wisdom should have known better, also put in a claim. Zeus was far too well acquainted with the female gender to judge this contest, so he sent them down to Mount Ida, recommending one of the sons of King Priam of Troy, Paris (one of mythology's regiment of abandoned princes who was posing as a shepherd), as an excellent judge of beauty. Somewhat startled at the sudden overpopulation of goddesses in his small glade, Paris balanced the golden apple in his hand as he listened in awe to the details of the beauty contest, which largely featured bribes. Hera promised him power over Europe and Asia; Athena, victory against the Greeks, and Aphrodite, with a little smile, offered the most beautiful woman in the world. Paris broke all speed records giving Aphrodite the apple. After dropping by the palace in Troy (where he was inexplicably welcomed), he sailed away to collect his reward.

Neither Aphrodite nor Paris worried for a moment about the fact that the most beautiful woman in the world was the aforementioned Helen, the wife of King Menelaus of Sparta. When Paris and Helen fled, Menelaus called in all Helen's former suitors who had sworn to uphold him in quarrels concerning her, and the Trojan War began.

Aphrodite spent a good deal of time causing princesses to fall in love with handsome strangers bent on projects prejudicial to the interests of the girls' fathers, who of course were kings. When Jason of Thessaly was sent to Colchis by his Uncle Pelias, who had usurped his brother's throne and hoped to dispose of the rightful heir, to retrieve the Golden Fleece, he asked permission of the king of Colchis to remove the Golden Fleece from the grove in which it hung. It was immediately obvious to men and gods that the king was not going to consent. So the goddess Hera, who sponsored Jason's quest, asked Aphrodite to intervene. The love goddess made the king's daughter Medea fall in love with Jason, and she became an enthusiastic partisan of his.

Aphrodite's busy schedule of involving men and gods in amorous turmoil did not mean that she herself was immune to the tender passion. Various stories are told of the handsome young man Adonis, but all agree that Aphrodite loved him passionately and grieved deeply when he died young of a wound received while hunting a boar, who hunted him back.

Aphrodite was credited with many affairs and many children. She fell in love with Anchises, a young cousin of Priam, King of Troy. The result of their liaison was Aeneas, whom she guided out of the burning city of Troy and on his route to Italy. The Romans, who claimed their descent from Aeneas, had much more to say about this particular story than did the Greeks, so we will return to Aeneas later.

Aphrodite's husband was the homely but highly-skilled Hephaestus, god of the fire and the forge. Some legends say this marriage was a punishment Aphrodite received for making the gods take part in so many undignified amours. This may have been fit punishment for her, but it was often rather hard on him. Although married to Hephaestus, Aphrodite bore Aeneas to Anchises, and Eros to Ares, the war god.

Despite her indisputable transgressions, Aphrodite, like the other gods, was worshipped in her magnificence. The *Homeric Hymn to Aphrodite* says: "I sing praise to stately and beautiful Aphrodite, crowned in gold, who holds the ramparts of sea-girt Cyprus . . . all the gods gape in amazement at the glory of violet-crowned Cytherea." Empedocles (*Fragment* 22) gets right to the heart of the matter: "Do you not see how mighty is the goddess Aphrodite? She sows and gives that love from which all we upon this earth are born."

ROMAN VENUS

Evidently originating in Ardea and Lavinium in central Italy, the Roman Venus began as a nature goddess associated with the arrival of spring who was grand patroness of gardens and vineyards. Since she was also in charge of love and beauty, she was, as might have been expected, the bringer of joy to gods and humans. As we have learned to expect in Rome, Venus had several titles. As Venus Genetrix, she was worshiped as the mother of the hero Aeneas, the founder of the Roman people; as Venus Felix, she was the bringer of good fortune; as Venus Victrix, the bringer of victory; and as Venus Verticordia, the protector (strangely enough) of feminine chastity.

She had numerous practical and homely duties and titles that would never have suited Greek Aphrodite. In 390 BCE the Romans were so soundly beaten at the river Allia by invading Gauls that they rushed back into the city without even closing the gates, and did not stop running until they reached the fortified citadel on the Capitoline Hill. Here they were besieged by the Gauls, and things became so desperate that Roman women gave their hair for bowstrings. Later, when the trouble was over, this sacrifice was commemorated by a dedication to Venus Calva—that is, Venus the Bald (Servius *Ad Aenean,* 1.720). As Rome remained standing rather than turning into a smoldering ruin, Venus evidently accepted this in the spirit in which it was meant. After all, for many years she had been accepting tributes in the small round temple of Venus Cloacina—Venus of the Sewer.

Many stories told of Venus, as is the case with the other gods, are those told of her Greek counterpart. However, the poet Vergil in his *Aeneid* added several of his own, concerned, as might be expected, with her struggles to protect her son Aeneas from the machinations of Juno. Juno hated all Trojans, evidently because she had never forgotten that golden apple, and she had a special prejudice against any offspring of Venus, who had been responsible for so many of Jupiter's failings. The Fates had decreed that

Aeneas would escape the destruction of Troy to be the ancestor of Rome, and the Fates, as the gods sometimes learned to their cost, always had their way. Juno, however, who was not only cow-eyed but also bullheaded, thought there must be an exception to every rule. After Aeneas had wandered about the Mediterranean for years trying to find out where he was going (the great gods who directed him to seek a new home were a bit stingy with directions), the little Penates (gods specific to a household or place) told him he was supposed to go to Italy. After several missed starts it looked as though he was about to get there when Juno bribed Aeolus, King of the Winds, to stir up a stupendous storm and shipwreck him on the coast of Africa, close to her city of Carthage, which was ruled by a young, beautiful widow named Dido. Venus, who had a fair idea of what Juno was trying to accomplish, disguised herself as a huntress and met Aeneas as he set out along the coast trying to get his bearings. She told him where he was and who was nearby, then thoughtfully concealed him and his companion Achates in a cloud of mist so that they could drift into Carthage and spy out the land before they were discovered. The Carthaginians and their queen did not notice this odd meteorological phenomenon, perhaps because they were too busy greeting some of Aeneas' men who had gotten separated from him in the storm. During these greetings Venus dissolved the cloud, and revealed Aeneas bathed in her own glow. Dido was suitably impressed, but to make sure that she fell in love with him Venus sent her mischievous little archer son Cupid, disguised as Aeneas' son Iulus, to the banquet the queen gave for the strangers. Needless to say Dido never had a chance, and she not only protected Aeneas during his stay in Carthage, but committed suicide when he, citing duty, left for Italy. Venus, who never worried about such casualties, moved on to sweet-talk various gods into helping her defend Aeneas and confound his enemies in Italy. She used all her winsome beauty and persuasiveness on the gods, and all her clever ruses on the goddesses, to achieve these ends. Thus, according to Vergil, the Romans had excellent reasons to call her the Mother of Rome.

III.10 ATHENA, GODDESS OF WISDOM

Athena was the Greek goddess of wisdom, the arts, handicrafts, and almost everything else that took a great deal of intelligence, as only Apollo among the Olympians came close to rivaling her in that admirable quality. As we have mentioned before, she was the daughter of Zeus alone.

"The city shall be safe."

After loving Metis (Wisdom), he began to fear that this consort would bear an offspring he could not control and swallowed his unfortunate inamorata. Later he developed a headache and the ever-helpful blacksmith god Hephaestus split his skull open. Thanks to this extreme surgical technique Athena emerged, fully grown and wearing armor. This might have been a sad omen of what her major occupation would be, but, though fierce and brave in battle, she was interested only in wars to defend the state and home. As she was Zeus' favorite child and was allowed to use his weapons, including his thunderbolt, her efforts in that direction were highly effective. Athena also wore upon her breastplate the aegis, a protective device that was originally associated with Zeus, but later the sole property of Athena. This shining shield became even more powerful when she received the snake-covered head of Medusa to fasten in the middle of it.

One legend says that Medusa acquired that snake-covered head because of hubris, which the Greek gods considered the greatest of all Cardinal Sins and of which Athena, as the story of Medusa indicates, took a particularly dim view. (Hubris consisted of an overweening arrogance concerning one's own outstanding qualities combined with the incredible stupidity required to challenge the gods with those qualities. Admittedly a lovely specimen, Medusa had compared herself in beauty to Athena with appalling results.) Athena was often the patroness of heroes; without her Odysseus would never have made it home to Ithaca in the face of Poseidon's wrath. (For that matter, he would probably never have made it through the Trojan War or invented the Trojan Horse without her assistance.) Her interest in the male sex was purely maternal, however, as she was foremost among the three virgin Goddesses unimpressed by the wiles of Aphrodite. Thus she was known as the Maiden, Parthenos. From this word was taken the name of the most important Temple dedicated to her, the Parthenon of Athens. Her immunity to the tender passion did not make her any less vain of her looks than other females, however: she invented the flute but threw it away because her face was distorted when she played it. Athens was of course her namesake and her city, and the olive she created in the contest with Poseidon her tree. The owl evidently gained its reputation for wisdom solely because it was her bird; under careful observance, owls exhibit no special signs of intellectual acumen.

ROMAN MINERVA

The Roman goddess Minerva or Menerva, like Jupiter and Juno, the other two members of the Capitoline Triad, was evidently of Etruscan origin. Since she was the daughter of Jupiter and Juno and the virgin goddess of wisdom, presiding over learning, all handicrafts, inventions, arts, and sciences, she was equated to Athena. As usual the Romans gave Minerva many attributes and names. As Minerva Victrix she was goddess of war. As Minerva Medica she was patroness of physicians. As she was also the inventor of numbers and musical instruments, Ovid had good reason to call her the "goddess of a thousand works (*Fasti* 3.833)." Like most of the Roman gods, she spent more time working and less time interacting with individual mortals than did her Greek counterpart. Minerva was goddess of wisdom and learning, meditation, inventiveness, accomplishments, the arts, spinning and weaving, and commerce. Possibly because of all these spheres of influence, Minerva has many aspects, attributes, names, and epithets.

III.11 HERMES, MESSENGER GOD

The *Homeric Hymn to Hermes* says that on Mount Cyllene in Arcadia Maia bore an amazing son, a cunning robber, a cattle driver, a bringer of dreams, a watcher by night, a thief at the gates, one who would do awesome deeds among the deathless gods (*Homeric Hymn* 4).

When Hermes was born, Maia placed the infant in his cradle, but he escaped and went out looking for amusement. Putting his divine attribute of speed to good use, he ran to Thessaly, where his brother Apollo had the Golden Oxen of the Sun grazing. Like any baby, he had a taste for

Swift and young and daring.

pretty things, so he helped himself to a number of the graceful creatures and concealed them in a cave near Pylos. While he was watching his stolen herd, he discovered a tortoise in the cave, and killed it. Using one of the cow's intestines and the tortoise's shell, he made the first lyre. Apollo complained to Maia that her son had stolen his cattle, but by that time Hermes had already curled himself up in his baby blankets, carefully concealing his new lyre under the covers. Maia refused to believe Apollo's story, and the infant prodigy Hermes, who added speech to his unusual early accomplishments, asked what cows might be. When the furious Apollo took the whole affair to Mount Olympus, Zeus showed a tendency to side with Apollo. Hermes then began to play music on the lyre he had invented. Apollo, the god of music, fell in love with the instrument and offered to exchange the cattle for the lyre. So Hermes was out of trouble and into a running start in his divine specialties.

With his amazing speed, it was no surprise that Hermes was made the messenger of the gods. Trade was another of his specialties, so he was dear to merchants. Thieves also prayed to him, and although the cynical say that the merchants behaved so much like thieves that he got mixed up with both of them, his attribute of speed and his own activities probably had more to do with this.

In his role as the messenger of the gods, and especially as conductor of the souls of the dead to the world below (which duty gave him the title of "Psychopompos—conductor of the soul"), Hermes carried the caduceus, which was given him by Apollo in exchange for yet another musical instrument, the pipes. The caduceus was a magic wand which exercised influence over the living and dead, and bestowed wealth and prosperity.

In its oldest form it was a rod ending in two prongs twined into a knot (probably an olive branch with two shoots, adorned with ribbons or garlands), for which, later, two serpents, with heads meeting at the top, were substituted. The poets explained the change with a story of Hermes finding two serpents thus knotted together while fighting; when he separated them with his wand, crowned by the serpents, it became the symbol of the settlement of quarrels. Hermes' well-known attire was completed by Zeus when he appointed his swift son as herald, or messenger of the gods. For his new appointment Zeus outfitted him with his well-known flat-crowned winged hat and his sandals with wings. Evidently as a final touch he added the wings to the caduceus and gave that to Hermes also. Zeus smiled on his newly-promoted son, but warned him that in the future he must respect property rights, refrain from telling outright lies, and safeguard travelers and commerce (Graves *The Greek Myths* 17). Hermes promised, smoothly and a little too quickly, to do all this.

In addition to a career in larceny grand and not so grand, Hermes, who evidently evolved from a pre-Hellenic fertility cult (Graves *The Greek Myths* 17) had a love life which staggers the imagination. We shall blushingly take a look at only a few of the foremost of his offspring.

While tending curly-fleeced sheep in the service of a mortal man, Hermes wed the daughter of Dryops, and she bore to him a son who from his birth was unusual, having goat's feet and two horns—a noisy, merry, laughing child. His nurse took one look at his leering face and full beard and fled. "Then Hermes took him in his arms with a glad heart" (*Homeric Hymn 19 to Pan*). This remarkable offspring was the great goat-god Pan, who became the deity of herdsmen and the companion of nymphs and satyrs, of whom he was chief. He danced and played upon the panpipes, or syrinx, a musical instrument so named because it had been made from reeds which had once been a maiden of that name. Syrinx had fled from Pan's wooing and prayed to be turned into a bed of reeds. When she got her wish, Pan fashioned his pipes from the reeds.

A very important but confusing offspring of Hermes was a daughter, Eleusis, borne to him by Daeira, an underworld goddess (her name also appears as a title of Persephone) who in most tales was a daughter of Oceanus who evidently represented some source of freshwater like her brother-rivers and sister-clouds. Therefore she was probably portrayed in the Eleusinian Mysteries as the goddess of grain-nourishing groundwater which Hermes (her consort) brought up from the Underworld every spring in the company of Persephone. (Pausanias *Description of Greece* 1.38) Some say her name is probably a title for Hecate or Persephone, and that Eleusis was not a daughter but a son. Whatever the facts about her mother and her gender may have been, Eleusis, the patron-goddess of the Eleusinian Mysteries and the goddess of the town of Eleusis, was one of the many attendants of Demeter.

Strangest of all Hermes' children is the son of Hermes and Aphrodite, Hermaphroditos. Hermaphroditos was born of Hermes and Aphrodite and received a name which is a combination of those of both his parents. He combined their physical aspects as well. Some said that he was born with a physical body which was a combination of that of a man and that of a woman. Some take that to mean that he has a body which is beautiful and delicate like that of a woman, but has the masculine quality and vigor of a man. But there are some who declare that such creatures of two sexes are monstrosities, and that they have the quality of presaging the future, sometimes for evil and sometimes for good. (Diodorus Siculus *Bibliotheca Historica* 4.6.5)

The Roman poet Ovid, who sees the romantic in every situation, however fantastic, says that Hermaphroditos had the bad luck to take a swim in the pool of Salmacis, where a nymph of the same name lived. When he refused her love, she clung to him and prayed to whatever mischievous gods might be listening that the two of them would be joined forever. When Hermaphroditos emerged from the pool, he had the characteristics of both a man and a woman.

In a nasty little revenge venture he prayed to his powerful parents that all men who swam in this accursed pool should suffer this same fate. (Ovid *Metamorphoses* 4.285) (If the men of the area were unkempt and somewhat smelly, who can blame them? Bathing in this pool, or any pool, may have seemed too great a risk to take.)

As in the case of the other gods, where Hermes found the time for all this dallying is a mystery. He had a full schedule caring for the globe-trotting travelers, guiding souls to Hades, keeping merchants on their toes, and carrying Zeus' messages all over the universe (not to mention dealing with the petitions no doubt directed to him by various and sundry merchants and thieves).

All this notwithstanding, Hermes, the beautiful wing-sandaled thief, had his good side. *Homeric Hymn* 18 calls him the "luck-bringing messenger of the deathless gods, the giver of grace and good things." He is linked with the gentle Hestia as one who is kind to poor mortals. "And you, slayer of Argus, Son of Zeus and Maia, messenger of the blessed gods, bearer of the golden rod, giver of good, be favorable and help us, you and Hestia, the worshipful and dear. Come and dwell in this glorious house in friendship together; for you two, well knowing the noble actions of men, aid their wisdom and their strength (*Homeric Hymn* 29).

ROMAN MERCURY

Mercury, son of Jupiter and Maia, was the Roman god of trade, profit, and commerce. His name is possibly derived from the Latin *merx* or *mercator,* a merchant. Merchants prayed to this overseer of trade and profit in order to attract good business. Originally the deity of traders in corn (by which term the Romans meant virtually any seed crop with a hard surface), he became the guardian of travelers and the messenger of the gods. Of course the Romans gave him at least one extra name, so he is known also as Alipes ("winged foot"). Strangely the sacred animal of this handsome, quick-footed thief was the chicken, and he is sometimes depicted with one. He resembled not only the Greek god Hermes but also the Etruscan Turms. Like Hermes, he is dressed in a wide cloak, wearing *talaria* (winged sandals) and *petasus* (winged hat) and carrying the *caduceus* (the staff with two intertwined snakes which the Romans said had power over sleeping, waking, and dreams). He also carries a purse or moneybag (a symbol of his connection with commerce).

Vergil describes Mercury when as messenger of the gods he was preparing to take Aeneas a rebuke from Jupiter concerning his dalliance with Queen Dido in Carthage, as Jupiter wanted Aeneas to go on to Italy and found Rome. First Mercury donned his golden, winged sandals, then took his caduceus, with which Vergil says he summoned souls from Orcus, sent others to Tartarus, lulled men to sleep or wakened them, and opened the eyes of the dead (*Aeneid* 4.239–44). Mercury, Vergil says, is "golden-haired and magnificent in his youth" (*Aeneid* 4.559), splitting the winds with his passage, then hovering on splendid wings above the earth, before he plunges down in awesome flight (*Aeneid* 4.245–46,

252–57). He promptly appears in all his splendor before the shocked Aeneas, to whom he gives a terse and effective command to end his dalliance with Queen Dido and to depart immediately for Italy.

III.12 HEPHAESTUS, GOD OF FIRE AND FORGE

Hephaestus, the lame god of fire and the god of volcanoes, was very early associated with the blacksmith's fire. He became the patron of all craftsmen, especially those working with metals, and was worshiped in manufacturing centers. Although he was the son of Zeus and Hera or, in some accounts, of Hera alone, Hephaestus, even more than Hestia, found himself ill at ease on Mount Olympus. Not only did he tend, like her, to simple straightforward behavior rather than the Byzantine plots of other Olympians, but he wasn't even good-looking. In stark contrast to the golden athletic perfection of his Olympian siblings, Hephaestus was generally represented as a sturdy and muscular man with a thick neck and hairy chest who, because of a shortened, lame leg and club foot, supported himself with the aid of a crutch. This humble hardworking god most often was shown dressed in a ragged sleeveless tunic and woolen hat, an ensemble in which no other Olympian deity would ever have appeared.

"I will bring him."

Some legends state that he was so ugly and unappealing at birth that Hera, his mother, threw him from the walls of Olympus into the sea, where he was rescued by the sea nymph Thetis. After Hera saw the lovely jewelry he made for Thetis at his forge, she insisted that he return to Mount Olympus to ply his trade. Never in her divine arrogance having paused to consider whether those she had injured in the past might be less than pleased with her autocratic commands, Hera delighted in a very beautiful golden throne which Hephaestus made for her. When she sat on it, however, it entrapped her, making her a prisoner. The Olympian gods pleaded with Hephaestus to release Hera, but he refused. Zeus, to no one's surprise, resorted to trickery. He sent Dionysus, the god of wine, to offer his brother some of his most outstanding vintage. Hephaestus received his initiation into the joys of the grape, and, rendered affable and obliging by his drinking, then mounted a donkey and, accompanied by Dionysus, rode back to Mount Olympus. Some say that before releasing Hera however, Hephaestus insisted upon being given the beautiful Aphrodite as his bride, a reward which often proved to be a punishment in itself.

However difficult his relationship with his mother might have been, Hephaestus argued for her when Zeus hung her in chains for rebelling against him. Not only did this intervention bring no help to Hera, it bought Hephaestus another swift descent from Olympus. This time Zeus threw him over the wall, and he landed on hard earth, breaking both his legs. He was eventually pardoned, but he was lame and, perhaps understandably, ill-tempered. As we have seen in previous stories, his temper was scarcely improved by his marriage to Aphrodite, who had not one trace of fidelity or constancy in her dazzling body.

As divine craftsman-in-chief Hephaestus manufactured wonderful articles from many materials, though his favorite was metal. His masterpieces included the palaces of gods atop Mount Olympus and the thunderbolts and scepter of Zeus as well as the weapons and accoutrements of most of the other gods. However, he spent little time on Mount Olympus unless he was actually working there. He was associated throughout Greek history with several volcanoes, especially Mount Etna in Sicily, and he preferred to ply his craft under his favorite volcano with help from the Cyclopes, who were his workmen and assistants. There he made the chariot (or according to some, the golden cup or goblet), which the sun god Helios rode across the sky, Athena's shield or aegis, and the arrows of Eros, the god of love. He also made accoutrements for heroes, among which were various articles for Heracles and the wonderful armor of Achilles which Homer takes great pains and many lines of the *Iliad* to discuss. To help him and his Cyclopes with all these commissions Hephaestus made a set of golden maidens who moved and did his bidding.

Prometheus stole the fire that he gave to man from Hephaestus' forge, and, perhaps because of this, Zeus commanded Hephaestus to create the first woman, Pandora, who, according to that old misogynist Hesiod, brought all sorts of catastrophes upon mankind.

It was also Hephaestus who, following Zeus' instructions, reluctantly chained Prometheus to the rock in Mount Caucasus with the help of Cratos (Power) and Bia (Violence):

> "Against my will, no less than yours, I must rivet you with brazen bonds ... Such is the prize you have gained for your championship of man."
> ([Hephaestus to Promethus] Aeschylus *Prometheus Bound* 20]
>
> Hephaestus: Oh handicraft that I hate so much!
>
> Cratos: Why hate it? Your craft is not to blame for these present troubles
>
> Hephaestus: Nevertheless, I wish it had fallen to another's lot!
> (Aeschylus *Prometheus Bound* 45)

Hephaestus was one of the very small minority of deities who were for the most part kind and gentle; thus he was beloved on earth. He and Athena were especially important to cities, where Hephaestus protected the smiths and Athena the weavers. The people revered and paid homage to these important deities. "Sing, clear-voiced Muses, of Hephaestus renowned for inventions. With bright-eyed Athene he taught glorious arts throughout the world to men, who before he came dwelled in mountain caves like wild beasts. Now that they have learned crafts through Hephaestus the brilliant worker, they live a peaceful easy life in their own houses the whole year round" (*Homeric Hymn* 11.1–7).

ROMAN VULCAN

The Roman fire god Vulcan, also called Mulciber, was very old. His Volcanal altar was one of the most ancient religious centers of Rome, and his festival, the Vulcanalia, dated back to the ancient Roman kingdom. He was the son of Jupiter and Juno, two of the Capitoline Triad, and the husband of Venus. Although he was the divine craftsman who made art, arms, and armor for gods and heroes, Vulcan seems to have originated as a god of volcanoes; thus the Romans were never as comfortable with him as the Greeks were with Hephaestus. With a wary eye on the destructive nature of his fiery power, the Romans tended to build his temples outside of town. Yet in the pious hope of obtaining his protection in averting fires, they dedicated numerous shrines or altars to him in places where fires were most feared, such as areas near volcanoes and where grain was stored, especially at the port of Ostia. He was the protector of smiths, and was normally depicted as a bearded man, dressed as a worker and carrying the utensils of a smith.

The Romans said that his fiery workshop was inside the volcano Mount Etna on the island of Sicily. There Vulcan with his helpers, the one-eyed Cyclopes and the golden maidens he had crafted, created his magnificent works.

He was linked with several primary goddesses, including Maia (as another Earth Mother) and Vesta, in her role as earth goddess. In addition to his ill-starred marriage to Venus, he had short-term relationships with other females. His offspring seemed generally to have been monstrous, such as the giant Cacus. Cacus, who had been half man and half something too monstrous to be described, had belched forth fire which he obtained from his father and proved to be a real nuisance to the very early people of central Italy until he made the fatal mistake of rustling some cattle belonging to Heracles (Vergil *Aeneid* 8.185–267).

Vulcan was sad about the death of his son Cacus and greatly displeased with the activities of Venus. In spite of her scandalous behavior, Vulcan wished to please his beautiful wife, who could be incredibly winsome when she chose. As a result of this wish combined with his sympathy for a harassed warrior, he outdid his usual superb craftsmanship when Aeneas went into his life-or-death struggle with the forces of the Italian warrior chief Turnus. Vergil devotes more than one hundred twenty lines in Book 8 of the *Aeneid* to the helmet gushing flame, the sword-blade edged with fate, and the blood-red bronze breastplate which Vulcan made for Aeneas, before carefully describing the giant shield on which he depicted the future history of Rome (*Aeneid* 8.608–731).

IV. THE TWO GREAT EARTH GODS

Although Greek Demeter was a sister of Zeus and company, and Roman Ceres was a member of the Di Consentes, both generally appear in mythology as earth goddesses, perhaps because they are so closely connected with agriculture.

IV.1 DEMETER, GODDESS OF AGRICULTURE

"All things shall grow."

In Greek mythology Demeter, the daughter of Cronus and Rhea and sister of Zeus, was goddess of agriculture and civilized life. With such a pedigree one might expect her to rank among the twelve great Olympians, but neither Homer nor Hesiod places her there; she is simply the great, good, and sorrowing grain goddess. (After all, being a female associated with the productivity of the soil, she was about as chthonic as one could be.) Her name has been explained as (1) grain-mother, from the Cretan form of wheat, barley, or (2) earth-mother in the Doric form. Her influence, however, was not limited to grain, but extended to livestock and fruits of the earth in general with the curious exception of the bean, the use of which was forbidden at Eleusis, and for the protection of which a special patron was invented. Her attributes are what might be expected: ears of corn, the poppy, the mystic basket (*calathus*) filled with flowers, and grain and fruit of all kinds, especially with the pomegranate. The cow and the pig are her favorite animals, the latter because of its productivity and the cathartic properties of its blood. Sacred to her, in addition to a grand array of livestock and agricultural products, are the poppy, asphodel, narcissus (which Persephone was gathering when carried off by Hades) and the crane, which is an indicator of the weather. As a chthonic divinity she is often accompanied by a snake.

The rituals concerning her, among the most important in Greece, were closely linked with her children, one of whom is her son Plutus. Hesiod says that "Demeter, the shining goddess, was joined in sweet love with the hero Iasion in a field in the fertile countryside of Crete, and brought forth Plutus, a kindly god who moves across both land and the wide sea; he bestows great wealth on those who find him" (*Theogony* 969–974). Homer adds a bit about Demeter's short-term consort: "So when Demeter fell in love with Iasion, and yielded to him in a thrice-ploughed fallow field, Zeus soon heard of it and killed Iasion with his thunderbolts" (*Odyssey* 5.125). (If any one should wonder just who this short-lived lover of the goddess may be, Apollodorus [*Bibliotheke* 3.138] says that this Iasion, lover of the great goddess, is the son of Zeus and Electra, but this is only one of six versions of Iasion's ancestry.) Both Homer and Hesiod place Demeter's brief romance in Crete.

Whatever the details may have been, the result was Plutus, the Greek god who personifies wealth. His attributes are a cornucopia and a basket filled with ears of corn. According to an extant but little regarded comedy of Aristophanes, the *Plutus*, Zeus blinded him because he distributed his gifts without regard to merit. At Thebes there stood a statue of Fortune holding the child Plutus in her arms; at Athens he was similarly represented in the arms of Peace; at Thespiae he was represented standing beside Athena the Worker. Elsewhere he was represented as a boy with a cornucopia.

Both Plutus and his father Iasion play their parts in Demeter's great ritual, the Eleusinian Mysteries, but they were little known outside the Mysteries. Evidently the central feature of her cult, and the cause of her eternal sorrow, was the story of her daughter Persephone. We have already seen that Persephone, daughter of Demeter and Zeus, was carried off by Hades to the Underworld. Demeter, wild with grief and showing the typical divine disregard for consequences, gave no fruitfulness to the earth, which promptly grew barren. To make matters worse, on finding a portion of Persephone's girdle, Demeter cursed the earth and the green plants all withered. Wandering across the wasteland she had created, ever searching for her daughter, Demeter came to Eleusis. Disguised as an old woman named Deo, she arrived at the house of Celeus at Eleusis, where she was hospitably received. The family invited the goddess to stay for dinner and told her about their son and brother who was dying. Demeter gathered poppies, and upon seeing the child, kissed him on the lips to restore his vitality and secretly placed poppy juice in his milk. Later that night, intending to give him immortality, she re-formed him, and started to place him into the fire for purification. The boy's mother, understandably disturbed by the sight, intervened. Demeter revealed her radiant form to the mother, and admonished her for being so protective. The son did not receive immortality but grew up to teach cultivation of the soil.

Demeter continued to search for her daughter until finally the sun god Helios (or in some versions the spring Arethusa) finally told her the truth: that Persephone had become Queen of the Underworld, and the wife of Pluto. Demeter appealed to Zeus for her return, and Zeus, realizing that something must be done if man or beast was to survive, agreed on the condition that Persephone had not eaten any food in the underworld. Hades, who had feared Persephone might be taken from him, had offered her a pomegranate, known as the food of the dead, so she would be forced to return to him. So, as Persephone had accepted a pomegranate from Pluto, and tasted the pulp of its seed, she must reside with her mother no more than half of each year. The remaining time she must spend with her husband in Hades. Demeter restored fruitfulness to the earth, but only for that time that her daughter spent with her.

In Greek art, Demeter is made to resemble Hera, only more matronly and of milder expression; her form is broader and fuller. She is sometimes riding in a chariot drawn by horses or dragons, sometimes walking, sometimes seated upon a throne, alone or with her daughter. The Demeter of Cnidus in the British Museum, of the school of Praxiteles, apparently shows her mourning for the loss of her daughter.

The Greeks loved and venerated Demeter as giving and loving, not fierce. "Demeter Eleusinia, universal mother, Deo renowned and venerable . . . great nurse, all-giving, blessed and divine, lover of peace and nourisher of the corn. Beautiful queen, nurse of all mortals; glorious, bright, and kind, bright and holy in nature. To you belong all the flowers, and fruits lovely and green. Bright Goddess, come, bring summer's rich growth, peace, harmony and health, and with them the wealth we need" (*Orphic Hymn 40 to Demeter*).

ROMAN CERES

Ceres was the ancient Italian goddess of agriculture; she was also chief representative of the love a mother bears for her child. Her cult was closely connected with that of Tellus, the Goddess Earth. "Let Tellus, fertile in fruits and herds, present Ceres with a crown of wheat stalks; let the healthy waters and breezes of Jupiter nourish the offspring" (Horace *Carmen Saeculare* 29–32). The Romans gave Ceres credit for the development of agriculture, saying that she was first to gather the wild corn and show men how to prepare it, preserve it, and sow it. Fully aware that replacing the hunter's life with agriculture would lead people to a settled life in close proximity to each other, she also introduced laws, so that settlement of their inevitable squabbles would possess some justice and fairness. "Ceres was the first to turn the sod with the hooked plowshare; she first gave laws. All things are the gift of Ceres; she must be the subject of my song" (Ovid *Metamorphoses* 5.341–344).

Unlike Demeter, who never made the list of the Twelve Great Olympians, Ceres was a member of the Dii Consentes. In later mythology, she was the daughter of Saturn and Rhea, the consort and sister of Jupiter and mother of Proserpina (Persephone). Ceres is portrayed with a scepter, a basket with flowers or fruits, and a garland made of ears of corn.

Curiously enough, in spite of her presence among the Dii Consentes, Roman Ceres was specifically the goddess of the plebs, or common people. Various reasons for this have been suggested. One of the more convincing states that her ancient associations with agriculture and fertility made her a commonly worshiped deity among Latin farmers. The patricians, being a jealous lot, are even said to have imported the worship of the Magna Mater, Cybele of Asia Minor, so that they might have a goddess similar to Ceres for their own. (After all, according to Vergil [*Aeneid* 9] Cybele had given her holy forest in Asia Minor to build Aeneas' fleet for his journey to Italy, and generally assisted in the founding of Rome.)

Thus there came to be a triad on the Aventine hill more in tune with the common people than the lofty Capitoline Triad. Slowly the Aventine Triad of Ceres, the grain goddess, Liber, the god of masculinity and wine, and Libera, Liber's feminine counterpart, became identified with Demeter, Dionysus and Perserphone, and the story of the lost daughter became part of their story. Thus it was said that Hades kidnapped Ceres' daughter Proserpina, and Ceres was so grief-stricken that she refused to allow anything on earth to be beautiful or fruitful while Proserpina was underground, only allowing summer and harvest time when she had her daughter with her.

IV.2 DIONYSUS, GOD OF WINE

"I am young but strong."

According to Hesiod (*Theogony* 900–942), Zeus fell in love with Semele, daughter of Cadmus. Hera in her jealousy led the pregnant Semele to ask Zeus for a fatal favor: that she might see him in all his glory. No mortal woman could bear such a sight, and she was consumed in the resulting conflagration. Dionysus was only saved from being consumed along with his mother by the quick action of Zeus, who snatched her baby from her and sewed it into his side until it was ready to be born. (This bizarre incident led to worshippers addressing Dionysus as "the insewn."). "The Father of men and gods brought you to birth concealed from mankind and from Hera, at Nysa, a great mountain in far off Phoenice richly rich with forests, near the streams of Aegyptus (*Homeric Hymn to Dionysus* 11.7–9). Be kind, O Insewn god, Inspirer of frenzied women! We sing of you as we begin and as we end a strain, and no one who forgets you can remember holy song. And so, farewell, Dionysus, the Insewn, with your mother Semele whom men call Thyone (*Homeric Hymn to Dionysus* 11.17–21)."

Hera, who was never known to give up a project easily, was still jealous and arranged for the Titans to kill Dionysus. They ripped him into pieces, but his grandmother Rhea brought him back to life. After this Zeus made careful arrangements for his protection and turned him over to the mountain nymphs to be raised. (At this point some researchers insert Dionysus 1 and Dionysus 2, making him separate gods before and after all this unpleasantness. For our simple survey, one is enough, and sometimes more than enough.)

However much this story of his birth places him squarely in the Olympian family tree (and a typical Olympian fracas), Dionysus was not one of the Big Twelve, and the story persisted that he was not truly Greek at all, but imported. Some scholars have long suspected that Dionysus has two distinct origins, those being a fusion of a local Greek nature god and another more potent god imported rather late in Greek pre-history from Phrygia or Thrace. (See Dionysus 1 and Dionysus 2 above.) He was certainly multi-faceted enough to have two, or more than two, prototypes. He was not only the god of wine, agriculture, and fertility of nature, but also, as the inspirer of poetry or song, the patron god of the Greek stage, in whose honor some of the finest drama the world has seen was written and staged. "Hail, child of beautiful Semele! He who forgets you can never order sweet song" (*Homeric Hymn 7 to Dionysus* 58–59). In addition to this he was very important in the mystery religions, such as those practiced at Eleusis, where he was closely associated with Demeter and Persephone. Perhaps because of his connection with wine, he represented ecstasy, escape from the humdrum world through intoxication (physical or spiritual), and initiation into secret rites typical of mystery religions.

Those dealing with classical gods were always well-advised to tread warily, but Dionysus was more dangerous than most, as he had a dual nature, reflecting the powers of wine. While he could bring joy and ease from sorrow, he also inspired brutal, unthinking rage which could drive men (and women) mad.

No normal fetters could hold him or his followers. *Homeric Hymn* 7 tells the story of a set of ill-fated pirates who learned this. Dionysus was evidently loitering about the seashore without the drinking vessel, ivy wreath, grape vines, and the *thyrsos* (a long fennel stalk wrapped with ivy leaves and topped with what appears to be a pine cone) which were his usual accoutrements. Seeing a handsome young man in a rich purple robe on the shore, the pirates seized him and took him on board their ship, dreaming of the ransom sure to be paid for a king's son. Dionysus, who among other things had a nasty sense of humor, allowed them to lead him on board and sat smiling as they tried to tie him up with ropes which fell apart as they touched him. The helmsman of the ship cried out that this was a god, and they had best let him go and ask his pardon, but the captain was countenancing no such craven behavior. He ordered the sailors to put out to sea, but even as they did fragrant wine ran along the decks and grape vines grew from the masts. Before they had recovered from this sight, Dionysus changed himself into a roaring lion and charged them. The sailors ran and gathered around the helmsman who had had the right idea in the first place. As the lion Dionysus seized the captain, however, the sailors lost their nerve and dived into the sea. Dionysus changed them into dolphins and then rewarded the cautious helmsman with riches.

According to some myths, Dionysus, more gallant than many gods, rescued the Cretan princess Ariadne after she had been abandoned by Theseus on the island of Naxos. Ariadne had helped Theseus escape from her father's Minotaur and labyrinth, and, according to most of the stories, he sailed away from Naxos and left her sleeping. Dionysus rode to the rescue, probably in his chariot drawn by lions or leopards, which might have terrified the poor girl if he had not distracted her by presenting her with a golden crown studded with gems. Some say this gift had belonged to Thetis, and was a work of Hephaestus. However that may have been, the crown served as a wedding present. When Ariadne died, Dionysus took the crown and threw it up into the sky, where it remains fixed in the heavens as a constellation. (Other versions of the Ariadne myth are less cheerful, saying that she hanged herself in despair or was slain by Artemis.)

Dionysus is also one of the very few who were able to bring a dead person out of the Underworld. He went to that gloomy realm to find his mother Semele, whom he had never seen. He faced down Thanatos, the dreadful god of death, and brought his mother back to Mount Olympus. (We might think that for an immortal to face Thanatos was not so difficult, as he himself could not die—at least not permanently. Getting this Grim Reaper to hand over one of his flock, however, was no simple matter.)

Dionysus wished to reward King Midas for rescuing old Silenus, who had protected the god in his youth and then become the most enthusiastic consumer of his wares, when the old drunkard had staggered into the hands of mischievous peasants. As a result of Silenus' rescue Dionysus granted the king one wish. King Midas chose, despite the advice of Dionysus, the ability to change everything he touched into gold. He had great fun beautifying his surroundings until lunchtime came, when his food underwent the metallic makeover. He then begged Dionysus to relieve him of his folly, and the god, laughing, told him to bathe in the river Pactolus. Midas was relieved of his inconvenient gift, and the river still sparkles with gold.

These stories of his kindness, however, must be matched against the stories of how Dionysus, when he moved into a new city and was resisted, destroyed those who opposed him. Euripides' play *The Bacchae*, written while the playwright was in the court of King Archelaus of Macedon, is the most famous of these. In this play we see Dionysus as very destructive and his worship very dangerous. Scholars have speculated not unreasonably that in Macedon Euripides discovered a more extreme form of the religion of Dionysus than the rather restrained forms in Athens. (Perhaps we should note that the name of the play indicates not Dionysus but Bacchus, which in both Greece and Rome indicated a much more unsavory character than his other face, Dionysus or Liber. We might also remember that Hera, never giving up on any object of her vengeance, drove him mad now and again.)

In the play Dionysus returns to Thebes, which is said to be his birthplace, where his cousin Pentheus is king, to punish any in Thebes who deny that he is a god. Pentheus has been enraged by the worship of Dionysus and has forbidden it, but he cannot stop the women, even his mother Agave, from rushing into the wilderness with the Maenads (women under the orgiastic spell of Dionysus, crazy with wine, wearing fawn skins on their shoulders and carrying the thyrsos. It was said that in their madness they would rip apart and eat raw any animal they came upon). Dionysus lures Pentheus to the wilds where he is killed by the Maenads and then mutilated by Agave.

Dionysus was one of the most important gods in everyday life, not only because he was the guardian of an important crop, but also because he became associated with several key concepts. One was rebirth after death. (Here his dismemberment by the Titans and return to life is symbolically echoed in tending vines, where the vines must be pruned back sharply, and then become dormant in winter if they are to bear fruit in the spring.) Another concept is the idea that under the influence of wine, one could feel possessed by a greater power. Unlike the other gods Dionysus was within his believers, and he might make a man greater then himself and lead him to do (or to think that he could do) works which he otherwise could not.

The characteristics of Dionysus, god of wine, who popularly represents emotion and chaos, were sometimes contrasted to those of Apollo, who represents harmony, order, and reason (for this pleasing literary picture the ancients glossed over that bow-bending side of Apollo). However, Greeks thought of the two qualities as complementary: the two gods are brothers, and when Apollo at winter left for Hyperborea he would leave the Delphic Oracle to Dionysus. (When one thinks about it, the ravings of the Pythia, the Delphic priestess, sound more like the work of Dionysus than that of Apollo.)

We have seen that, after Hephaestus had taken revenge on his unloving mother Hera by imprisoning her on a golden throne, none of the Olympians could persuade him to return to Olympus to release her. Dionysus took the smith god some wine, and, after Hephaestus was intoxicated, took him back to Mount Olympus slumped over the back of a mule. Some say that while Hephaestus' two-edged reward for the release of Hera was the beautiful Aphrodite, Dionysus was rewarded by being made one of the Olympian Pantheon.

ROMAN LIBER/BACCHUS

The name of the Roman wine god Liber, like that of his counterpart deity Libera, is derived from the Latin word that meant "to set free." After the formation of the Aventine Triad, he absorbed the mythology of Dionysus. Liber may or may not have been the god of wine before this took place. (His feminine counterpart, as we have seen, through the identification of Ceres with Demeter wound up being equated to Persephone. Some claimed that Libera was once the counterpart of Ariadne, who was a goddess or demigoddess. If so, Ariadne disappeared from this tale as religion advanced.)

Liber himself never seems to have been viewed as particularly dangerous or subversive, being associated with growing vines or, at the outside, fertility in general, vegetable and human. His festival was a homey affair, at which old ladies sold honey cakes in the street. As in Greece however, his Bacchus persona was another matter. The Bacchanalia, orgies in honor of Dionysus, were introduced in Rome around 200 BCE. It took only fourteen years for thinking Romans to decide that these infamous celebrations, notorious not only for sexuality but also for criminality, should be stopped. The Roman Senate forbade them in 186 BCE. As happens so often in such cases, the legislation gave the legislators a comfortable feeling of having done the right thing, but had very little effect on the festivals.

Thus we bring to a close our brief view of the most widely known Greek and Roman deities. The ancients through many centuries observed the beautiful, mysterious and dangerous world around them and speculated about how it came to be and how its glories could be gained and its horrors avoided. They then bent their creative imaginations to the invention and the worship of supernatural beings who, they hoped, would have enough interest in mankind and enough control of natural phenomena to help them in their great struggle not only to survive and prosper, but also to beautify and enrich the world around them.

V. NOTES

CAMILLA

Camilla was an Italian princess whose father Metabus had been such a cruel king that his people, the Volscians, had risen against him. He had fled for his life carrying his tiny daughter in his arms. When he reached the flooding river Amasenus, he knew that the Volscians were not far behind him and that he could not swim across the river carrying the baby. He wrapped Camilla carefully in the bark of a cork oak tree and tied her to a huge battle spear of oak. As he prepared to throw the spear, he prayed to the forest goddess Diana to protect the child and promised that the child would be the servant of the goddess if she survived. The spear landed safely on the other side of the river, and Metabus swam across the water and escaped the pursuit with his little daughter.

While he lived the rest of his life as a shepherd in the forest, Metabus taught Camilla to worship Diana and to hunt with darts and slingshots. As Camilla grew older, she advanced to the weapons of war, which she used with appalling effectiveness. When the war between Aeneas the Trojan and the Italian prince Turnus began, Camilla, surrounded by a bodyguard of maiden warriors, joined Turnus and led the cavalry of the Volscians into battle. The Trojans were amazed by her beauty and grace, but they soon learned that she was dangerous. She killed many men in battle before she was killed by the Etruscan Arruns. The followers of Diana, who were incensed by her death, followed Arruns into a deserted valley and killed him.

CAPITOLINE HILL

One of the seven hills upon which Rome was built. The others were the Palatine, the Aventine, the Caelian, the Quirinal, the Viminal, and the Esquiline.

CHTHONIC DEITIES

Gods dwelling in or under the earth.

CIRCE AND MEDEA

These two devotees of the goddess Hecate were the two best-known great sorceresses of the ancient world. They were young and beautiful, which stands to reason, since a female of such great powers would be unlikely to go around as an old hag. Medea was the daughter of King Aeetes of Colchis, and the granddaughter of Helios, the sun god. She fell in love with the adventurer Jason and helped him steal the Golden Fleece from her father. A firm believer in the "all for love" philosophy and a bit short on moral fiber, Medea cut her younger brother Absyrtis in pieces to distract her father from pursuing her and her lover as they fled. Later in a similar manner she dispatched Pelias, the king of Iolcus who had usurped the throne belonging to Jason's father by a singularly underhanded method, to his exceedingly questionable eternal reward. Having made Iolcus too hot to hold them, Jason and Medea fled to Corinth, where, two offspring later, Jason was harebrained enough to plan to desert Medea and marry the daughter of Creon, King of Corinth. This bit of social climbing on his part not only brought his fiancee a fiery death, but caused Medea to kill her two children in order to punish him. Medea borrowed her grandfather Helios' chariot, fittingly drawn by winged dragons, and fled to Athens, where she married Aegeus, the old king of Athens, and bore him a son, Medus. She tried to trick old Aegeus into poisoning his son Theseus. When this did not work, she took her son and fled again, disappearing, to everyone's intense relief, from Greek literature.

Circe lived in the Mediterranean on an island named Aeaea. If this name sounds like a scream, it should. Circe whiled away her duller hours by turning any men who came her way into beasts–the four-footed kind. The poor fellows retained their reason but had inadequate voices to complain about their misfortunes. Anyone approaching the island too closely could hear the roars, oinks, and other assorted noises made by Circe's unwilling guests. At one point Picus, grandfather of King Latinus whom Aeneas met in Italy, wed Circe. After a pleasant honeymoon Circe in a fit of pique turned Picus into a woodpecker.

ORPHIC HYMNS

A collection of about eighty short poems of praise to various divinities, used in ritual and sacred practice for almost one thousand years, from 300 BCE to CE 500 in Thrace, Phrygia, Anatolia, and the rest of what we now call Asia Minor, as well as on the Greek mainland and islands. They take their name from Orpheus, the famous and probably legendary poet and musician who is credited with founding the Orphic religion, one of the major belief systems of the archaic Hellenistic world.

Each of the hymns is headed by "the fumigation of aromatics" which usually includes a short description of the herbs or substances used as a means of calling on the deity. After the gods might be presumed to be sniffing and hopefully listening, hymns were chanted by groups in sacred circles to invoke particular deities.

THEOGONY

A poem by Hesiod composed ca. 700 BCE. It describes the origins and family relationships of the Greek gods.

VERNAL EQUINOX

The equinoxes are the two days each year when the center of the sun spends an equal amount of time above and below the horizon at every location on earth. The word *equinox* derives from the Latin words *aequus* (equal) and *nox* (night). The autumnal equinox occurs in the autumn (in September in the Northern Hemisphere), the vernal equinox in spring (in March in the Northern Hemisphere).

BIBLIOGRAPHY

Beard, Mary, John North, and Simon Price. *Religions of Rome.* Cambridge: Cambridge University Press, 1998.

Colakis, Marianthe and Mary Joan Masello. *Classical Mythology and More: A Reader Workbook.* Wauconda, IL: Bolchazy-Carducci Publishers, 2007.

Graves, Robert. *The Greek Myths.* Harmondsworth, England: Penguin Books, 1955.

Harris, Stephen L. and Gloria Platzner. *Classical Mythology: Images and Insights.* New York: McGraw-Hill, 2003.

Kirkwood, G.M. *A Short Guide to Classical Mythology.* Wauconda, IL: Bolchazy-Carducci Publishers, 2003.

Morford, Mark and Robert Lenardon. *Classical Mythology.* 7th ed. Oxford: Oxford University Press, 2002.

Stern, Jacob (trans.). *Palaephatus: On Unbelievable Tales.* Wauconda, IL: Bolchazy-Carducci Publishers, 1996.

Williams, Rose. *Gods and Other Odd Creatures.* Austin, Texas: Cicada-Sun Publishers, 2007.

ANCIENT SOURCES

Aeschylus. *Prometheus Bound.*

Apollodorus. *Bibliotheke,* "The Library."

Aristophanes. *The Birds, Plutus.*

Cicero. *De legibus,* "Concerning the Laws."

Diodorus Siculus. *Bibliotheca Historica,* "Library of History."

Empedocles. *Fragment 22.*

Ennius. *Fragmentary Works.*

Euripides. *The Bacchae.*

Hesiod. *Theogony.*

Homer. *Iliad, Odyssey.*

Homeric Hymns.

Horace. *Odes; Carmen Saeculare,* "Secular Song."

Livy. *Ab Urbe Condita,* "From the Founding of the City."

Orphic Hymns.

Ovid. *Fasti,* "Festivals of the Roman Year"; *Metamorphoses,* "Transformations."

Pausanias. *Description of Greece.*

Plato. *Phaedrus.*

Servius, *Ad Aenean,* "To Aeneas."

Stesichorus. *Fragment 192: The Palinode.*

Vergil. *Aeneis,* "Aeneid."

(For texts with a Latin title, an English translation is provided).

PHOTOGRAPHY CREDITS

LATIN FOR THE NEW MILLENNIUM

The cutting-edge program for learning Latin and unlocking the wisdom of the ages from the Roman playwrights Terence and Plautus to the revolutionary thought of Copernicus and a heliocentric world.

Check out **WWW.LNM.BOLCHAZY.COM**

ENJOYED *THE ORIGINAL DYSFUNCTIONAL FAMILY?*

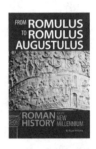

Then, you'll like its companion title—*The Clay-footed Superheroes: Mythology Tales for the New Millennium.* Greece gave the world its first widely-known superheroes whose achievements, foibles, and adventures will capture your imagination. Also check out *From Romulus to Romulus Augustulus: Roman History for the New Millennium.* Learn how this civilization came to dominate its world and remains the foundation of our own world. Learn about Rome's impact and Latin's role in medieval and Renaissance periods—read *From Rome to Reformation: Early European for the New Millennium.* Students love Rose Williams' works!

LATIN FOR THE NEW MILLENNIUM RECOGNIZES THAT STUDENTS LEARN FROM AND VALUE THE INTERNET!

So, *Latin for the New Millennium* provides a variety of online materials that not only complement your Latin lessons in the text but also encourage *active use of Latin* within *fun learning environments.*

QUIZ YOURSELF ONLINE

Check out *Looking at Latin* online—with over 6,000 questions covering all points of Latin grammar, you can build your Latin skills. Spend some time doing Latin online and watch your understanding of Latin grow!

SO, YOURS IS A MORE ADVENTUROUS BENT . . .

Bolchazy-Carducci Publishers sponsors a Latin-language guild, *Carpe Praedam* within the enormously popular on-line game, World of Warcraft™. Guild members currently include both teachers and students who use the game to *practice their conversational Latin skills while questing for treasure and honor.*

eClassics

YOU'D LIKE TO SHARE YOUR INSIGHTS ABOUT STUDYING LATIN AND THE CLASSICS?

You're invited to join hundreds on eClassics. Just like Facebook but for the classics! Just click on **eClassics**.

With online exercises, games, and virtual worlds, *Latin for the New Millennium* provides the contemporary learning tools students like.